A Souvenir of
Shelburne Museum

© 2005 Shelburne Museum, Inc.
First printing.

Cover: *The 1901 Round Barn Welcome Center and Circus Building (background).* Photo by Mac Carbonell.

Title Page: *The Museum grounds facing north.*

ISBN: 0-939384-30-2

Graphic Design
Vicky McCafferty.

Photography
Carolyn L. Bates, David Bohl, Paul O. Boisvert, Andrew Bordwin, Clive Boursnell, Ken Burris, Mac Carbonell, Andy Duback, Sanders H. Milens, Mark Sasahara, Larry Shutts, Jim Westphalen.

Writers
Sam Ankerson, Jean Burks, Henry Joyce, Chip Stulen.

Printed by
The Offset House, Essex, Vermont.

Published by
Shelburne Museum
P.O. Box 10
Shelburne, VT 05482
(802) 985-3346
www.shelburnemuseum.org

Table of Contents

Introduction

SHELBURNE MUSEUM is one of the finest, most diverse, and idiosyncratic museums of art and Americana. Electra Havemeyer Webb (1888-1960), daughter of European and Asian art collectors H.O. and Louisine Havemeyer, founded the Museum in Shelburne, Vermont in 1947. Possessed of an independent and confident eye, she began collecting in 1908 at the age of 19 and developed a passion for early-American vernacular forms — what she called "the beauty of everyday things."

Mrs. Webb was one of the pioneering collectors of folk art. She acquired quilts, weather vanes, trade signs, sculptures, paintings, furniture, decorative arts, and a dazzling array of 17th- to 20th-century artifacts. Today, over 150,000 works are exhibited at Shelburne Museum in 39 exhibition buildings on a 45-acre site.

Mrs. Webb worked with several prominent dealers and galleries, including the Downtown Gallery in New York City, but she also tirelessly explored the villages and countryside of New England for her acquisitions. Her country houses in Vermont and Long Island were the first homes for her collections, and she experimented there with creative exhibition ideas she later used at Shelburne Museum. A gift in 1946 of 28 horse-drawn carriages crystallized her decision to create "an educational project, varied and alive," and the Museum was born.

Mary Cassatt (1844-1926)
Louisine Havemeyer and her Daughter Electra
1895
Pastel on paper
H: 30 1/2", W: 24"
Museum purchase, 1996
27.3.1-49

Mary Cassatt was a close friend of the Havemeyers and advised on their collecting of modern French paintings. This remarkable portrait of two generations of influential women collectors hangs in the Electra Havemeyer Webb Memorial Building.

As enamored of iconic New England architecture as she was of art and artifacts, Mrs. Webb took the imaginative step of collecting 18th- and 19th-century buildings in which to display the new museum's holdings. Between 1947 and 1960, she relocated 20 historic structures to the Museum, including houses, barns, a meeting house, a one-room schoolhouse, a lighthouse, a covered bridge, and the 220-foot steamboat *Ticonderoga*. At the same time, she directed construction of new buildings and extensive landscape and garden design. What visitors experience at Shelburne Museum is entirely unique: remarkable collections exhibited in a village-like setting of historic architecture, accented by a pastoral landscape that includes over 400 lilacs, a circular formal garden, herb and heirloom vegetable gardens, and several perennial gardens.

The Museum continues to expand and evolve. New buildings, new acquisitions, and special exhibitions enhance Shelburne's collections and offer fresh perspectives on four centuries of art, history, and material culture. Moving into the 21st century and guided by Electra Webb's extraordinary legacy, Shelburne is a museum unlike any other.

Electra Havemeyer Webb, 1948.

The early-19th-century Blacksmith Shop being moved through Shelburne en route to the Museum in 1955.

Maker Unknown
Mary O'Connor
19th century
Carved and painted wood
H: 64", W: 21", D: 20"
Purchased from the Estate of J. Watson Webb, Jr., 2000
2000-24.1

This tobacconist figure was, in 1908, 19-year-old Electra Havemeyer's first folk art purchase.

The Museum's lilacs reach full bloom in May. There are over 400 in 90 varieties throughout the grounds.

Electra Havemeyer Webb Memorial Building and Impressionism

MRS. WEBB'S MOTHER, Louisine Havemeyer, was a close friend of American Impressionist painter Mary Cassatt, who encouraged Mrs. Havemeyer and her husband H.O. to buy French Impressionist pictures. Most of the Havemeyers' great collection — over 500 pictures — went to the Metropolitan Museum of Art in New York City, but their children inherited paintings as well. Mrs. Webb had intended to bring her inheritance to Shelburne Museum, and her children built the Electra Havemeyer Webb Memorial Building after her death to house the collection, which she had bequeathed to the Museum.

Among the highlights are five works by Claude Monet, three by Édouard Manet, seven by Edgar Degas, and four pastels and two prints by Mary Cassatt. They are superb examples of the best modern art between 1870 and 1900. Also in the building are works by 19th-century French painters Gustave Courbet, Jean-Baptiste-Camille Corot, and Charles-François Daubigny.

The pictures hang in six interiors moved from Electra and J. Watson Webb's 740 Park Avenue apartment. The English neoclassical-style rooms, designed by the New York firm Schmitt Brothers and completed in 1931, are fine examples of sophisticated 20th-century New York City interiors. At Shelburne, the best rooms from the triplex apartment survive with their original furnishings, including many excellent pieces of 18th-century English furniture.

Electra Havemeyer Webb Memorial Building.

The living room of Electra Webb's 1930s Park Avenue apartment features paintings by Monet, Manet, and Corot. It is one of six rooms from the apartment on view in the Memorial Building.

Édouard Manet (1832-83)
Au Jardin (In the Garden)
About 1870
Oil on canvas
Signed lower right: *Manet*
H: 17 ¹/₂", W: 21 ¹/₄"
Gift of Dunbar and Electra Webb Bostwick, 1981
27.1.1-200

The identity of the subjects in this early Impressionist painting is not known, but they were probably friends of the artist. The informality of the scene makes it a strikingly modern picture.

Édouard Manet (1832-83)
The Grand Canal, Venice (Blue Venice)
1875
Oil on canvas
Signed extreme right at bottom of pole: *Manet*
H: 23 ¹/₈", W: 28 ¹/₈"
Gift of Electra Havemeyer Webb Fund, Inc., 1972
27.1.5-30

Manet painted this picture on his visit to Venice in fall 1875. It is one of only two canvases he completed on that trip. The picture's strongly Impressionist style, with its sketch-like strokes of paint made to capture the water's moving reflections of light, is rare in Manet's work.

Edgar Degas (1834-1917)

L'École de Dance (The Dance Class)

1873-79

Oil and tempera on canvas

Signed lower right: *Degas*

H: 17 ¼", W: 23"

Gift of Electra Webb Bostwick, 1976

27.3.1-35A

This painting is the final work of a small group of pictures showing the same Paris rehearsal room at the rue Le Peletier Opéra. The picture was done in Degas' studio, where he worked from memory and from preliminary sketches of individual dancers. The picture was exhibited at the fourth Impressionist Exhibition in Paris in 1879.

Claude Monet (1840-1926)

Les Glaçons (The Ice Floes)

1880

Oil on canvas

Signed lower right: *Claude Monet 1880*

H: 38 ¼", W: 58 ¼"

Gift of Electra Havemeyer Webb Fund, Inc., 1972

27.1.2-108

Monet painted The Ice Floes *for submission to the government-sponsored Salon exhibition in 1880, but the picture was rejected because the pinks and blues were considered too unconventional. The colors, however, give a powerful sense of the melting ice in sunlight after France's record-setting freeze in the winter of 1879-80. The picture was exhibited at the seventh Impressionist Exhibition in 1882.*

Claude Monet (1840-1926)

Meules, Effet de Neige (Grainstacks, Snow Effect)

1891

Oil on canvas

Signed lower left: *Claude Monet 91*

H: 23", W: 39"

Gift of Electra Havemeyer Webb Fund, Inc., 1972

27.1.2-106

The painting is one of 14 grainstack views Monet painted in the fields around his house at Giverny that were included in the artist's spring 1891 Paris show. It was the first time he exhibited a series of pictures showing the same subject in different weather and light conditions.

Transportation

ALTHOUGH ELECTRA WEBB had been collecting for over 30 years, it was a 1946 gift from the estate of her in-laws, William Seward and Lila Vanderbilt Webb, of 28 elegant carriages that prompted her decision to create Shelburne Museum. Today, the collection of horse-drawn vehicles (which includes carriages, sleighs, stage-coaches, and commercial wagons) is the most comprehensive in America. The Museum's 225 vehicles are exhibited in two barns constructed on site, Horseshoe Barn and Horseshoe Barn Annex.

The Museum's railroad collections include the 1890s *Grand Isle* private rail car, a triumph of Gilded Age luxury with a mahogany-paneled interior, dining room, parlor, and three state-rooms. Attached to the private car is Locomotive 220, built in 1915, and adjacent to the train is the Town of Shelburne Railroad Station, which operated from 1890 to 1953 and was relocated to the Museum in 1959.

Gold satin-lined interior of the 1890 Berlin Coach, a jewel of the carriage collection and part of the 1946 gift from the estate of Dr. and Mrs. William Seward Webb.

Million and Guiet
Berlin Coach
Paris, France
1890
Painted wood, steel, patent leather, silk, brass, and glass
Gift of Vanderbilt Webb in memory of Dr. William Seward and Lila Vanderbilt Webb, 1946
40-V-48

The 1890 Shelburne Railroad Station.

Steamboat
Ticonderoga

THE 220-FOOT Lake Champlain steamboat *Ticonderoga* was commissioned by the Champlain Transportation Co. in 1905. It was built at the Shelburne Shipyard and launched into service August 6, 1906. It was the last of 29 steamers built for the lake and is the last walking beam side-wheel passenger steamer in existence. Today, the *Ti* is a fully restored National Historic Landmark.

Designed to carry nearly 1,100 passengers and all types of freight, the *Ticonderoga* operated as a day boat serving ports along both the New York and Vermont shores. Its massive coal-fired walking beam engine has a single vertical cylinder with a 52"-diameter piston weighing three tons and a stroke of nine feet. Although technically antiquated by 1906, this engine type had proven a reliable workhorse for the lake and was installed into the new steamboat.

To the passengers, however, the *Ticonderoga* was a modern, elegant steamer complete with carved and varnished woodwork, gilded stenciled ceilings, and electric lighting. The *Ti* served Lake Champlain's transportation needs for nearly five decades. Remarkably, it survived intact and unaltered through the all-encompassing technology shift from steam power to the internal combustion engine.

Since its last season under steam in 1953 and the subsequent monumental two-mile overland journey to the Museum grounds, the *Ticonderoga* has been a centerpiece of Shelburne Museum, where it portrays everyday life on a steamboat in 1923. Visitors fully explore its four decks, including the massive engine, the luxurious dining room, the captain's stateroom, and the splendid grand stair and stateroom hall. The promenade decks lead to the hurricane deck and a commanding view of the Museum from the pilot house.

Steamer *Ticonderoga*
Built: 1906
Purchased: 1951
Moved to the Museum: 1955
Length: 220 feet
Beam: 57.5 feet
Displacement: 892 tons

During the winter of 1954-55, when the frozen ground could support the 892-ton Ticonderoga *she was hauled on a double railway bed two miles to the Museum grounds, a remarkable engineering feat that took 65 days.*

The saloon deck. Through the generosity of Vermont philanthropists Lois McClure and her late husband, J. Warren McClure, the Ticonderoga was fully restored in the 1990s.

The grand stair on the Ticonderoga.

Lighthouse

The Colchester Reef Lighthouse was built in 1871 and operated on Lake Champlain just north of Burlington, Vermont until 1933. The two-story, six-room structure was the home and workplace for 11 successive lighthouse keepers and their families.

The lighthouse was dismantled and relocated to Shelburne Museum in 1952, joined three years later by the steamboat Ticonderoga. Lighthouse exhibitions survey Lake Champlain maritime history and the life of a lighthouse keeper.

Historic Houses

Each of the Museum's historic houses has its own distinctive style. The furnishings of Stencil House reflect the collecting taste of Electra Webb, and those of Prentis House are characteristic of her friend Katharine Prentis Murphy's interest in baroque furniture. Dutton House is shown as it was lived in between 1820 and 1830.

Stencil House (foreground), Prentis House, and the Colchester Reef Lighthouse (background) during the lilac bloom in May.

Stencil House

STENCIL HOUSE, built in 1804 in Sherburne, New York, was moved to Shelburne Museum in 1953. It was named for its outstanding floor-to-ceiling stenciled walls of the 1830s.

The parlor showcases the original stencils after extensive cleaning and restoration in 2001. The dining room walls were repainted to replicate the damaged original stencils.

Stencil House dining room.

On the stenciled parlor walls is a high-style English neoclassical gilded mirror frame. It is flanked on one side by a Massachusetts Windsor chair from about 1820 and on the other by a rare American marble-topped mixing table from about the same date. The New England maple tea table from the mid-18th century was bought from Connecticut antiques dealer John Kenneth Byard, who supplied several pieces for Stencil House.

Prentis House

PRENTIS HOUSE, named for distinguished collector and Shelburne Museum Trustee Katharine Prentis Murphy, was built in 1773 and relocated from Hadley, Massachusetts in 1955. Mrs. Murphy donated all the furnishings, which feature European and American baroque objects. The interiors reflect the collecting taste of the mid-20th century rather than furnishings appropriate to the 18th-century date of the house.

The Prentis House parlor as furnished in 1957 by Katharine Prentis Murphy. The faux black-and-white marble floor was added in 2001 to honor Mrs. Murphy, who used this decorative device in her re-creations of other historic house interiors.

The bedhangings in Prentis House's west chamber were made in 2001 by members of the New England chapter of the Embroiders' Guild of America.
They replicate the original 18th-century hangings, now preserved in storage.

Dutton House

DUTTON HOUSE, an example of continuous architecture reflecting use by several generations, was the first domestic building moved to the Museum, in 1950. Begun in 1782 in Cavendish, Vermont, it is named for the family that occupied it for 125 years. The interiors are furnished to the 1820s-'30s, when the Duttons ran a tavern in the building. The rooms feature a group of fine cast-iron stoves and several examples of Vermont-made furniture.

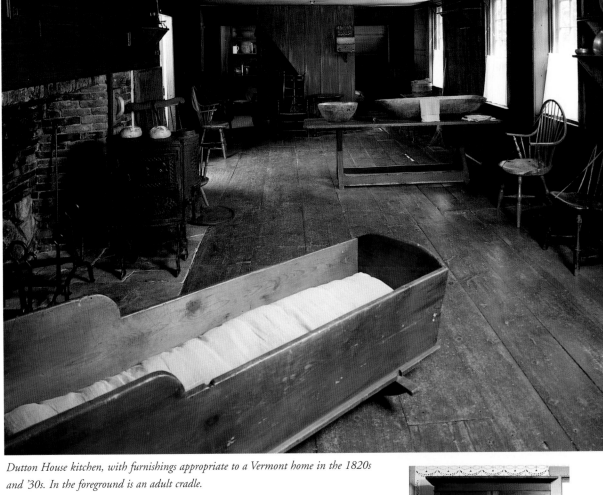

Dutton House kitchen, with furnishings appropriate to a Vermont home in the 1820s and '30s. In the foreground is an adult cradle.

Dutton House.

John Marshall (1787-1860)
Secretary
Royalton, Vermont
1825-30
Wood, glass, and brass
H: 76 3/4", W: 45 3/4", D: 21"
Gift of Norman Fowler, 2000
2000-17a-l

This superb Vermont-made piece was acquired by the Museum in 2000 and is exhibited in the Dutton House dining room.

Settlers' House and Barn

Education programs at Settlers' House help bring Vermont's frontier days to life.

SETTLERS' HOUSE is a living history exhibition comprising a two-room log house, a barn, an operating bake oven, and flax and vegetable gardens. Costumed interpreters recreate the experiences of daily life in the early days of Anglo settlement in Vermont (about 1795). Through Settlers' House, visitors gain an understanding of Vermont's agricultural heritage and early history.

Meeting House and Schoolhouse

The Museum's historic community buildings include a brick Meeting House (above) from Charlotte, Vermont, built about 1840, and an 1840 one-room schoolhouse from Vergennes, Vermont.

The schoolhouse features six rows of desks and lesson plans typical of the late 19th century written in chalk on the blackboard (right).

Variety Unit and Decorative Arts

SHELBURNE'S DECORATIVE ARTS collections are among the finest in America. The objects are showcased in Variety Unit, a brick farmhouse built about 1835 that is the only structure original to the Museum site. It is named Variety Unit for the extraordinary range of collections on view and for the sense of discovery that visitors experience as they wind through its rambling rooms and hallways. In many ways, Variety Unit is the soul of Shelburne Museum.

The first floor holds the Museum's primary decorative arts galleries and exhibits ceramics, glass, scrimshaw, trivets, food molds, and pewter, mostly created in Europe and America in the 18th and 19th centuries. The rich diversity of forms and surface patterns of these artifacts caught the eye of Mrs. Webb, who collected them primarily for their visual appeal.

The second floor houses antique dolls (among the premier museum collections of its kind in the United States), dollhouses, and European and American automata.

Attached to Variety Unit is the Toy Shop, featuring 19th-century toys made of wood, tin, and cast iron.

Mochaware and food molds on exhibit in Variety Unit.

Variety Unit was originally built as a farmhouse in Shelburne about 1835.

Operating American Flyer toy trains are on view in the Toy Shop, an annex of Variety Unit.

The mammoth jug room in Variety Unit holds a colorful collection of 19th-century English-made jugs in many sizes.

Ceramics

SHELBURNE MUSEUM'S broad collection of ceramics includes English Staffordshire, mocha-ware, and Chinese export porcelain. Outstanding examples are highlighted here.

Chelsea Manufactory
Swan-Shaped Tureens
Chelsea, England
1752-58
Soft paste porcelain
Left: H: 11", W: 16 3/4", D: 11"
Right: H: 18 1/2", W: 18 1/2", D: 11 1/2"
Gift from the Estate of Electra Havemeyer Webb, 1961
31.4-1a-b

These swan-shaped tureens were made in Chelsea, England (in an area that is now part of London) at a factory established in 1745 by French Huguenot silversmith Nicholas Sprimont. The underside of the taller tureen is painted with a red anchor over the glaze, an identification mark used by the factory only from 1752 until 1758.

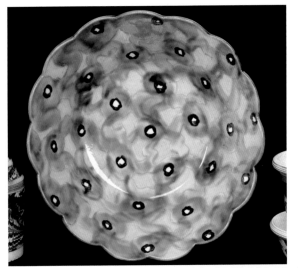

Josiah Spode II (1754-1827)
Compote
Staffordshire, England
1805-20
Pearlware with polychrome decoration
H: 5 3/4", Diameter: 10"
Museum purchase, 2004
2004-21

This whimsically decorated compote with a scalloped rim is representative of ceramics popular in the English and American market of the early 19th century.

Wedgwood Company
Two Compotes and a Covered Dish
Staffordshire, England
About 1810-20
Pearlware with luster glaze
Left: H: 8", W: 9 1/2", D: 6 1/2"
Center: H: 6", W: 7 1/4", D: 6 1/4"
Right: H: 8 1/4", W: 10", D: 5 7/8"
Museum purchase, 2004
2004-24.1, .2, and .3

These pieces are part of Wedgwood's rare Nautilus dessert service. Each form is modeled after a specific seashell, including the nautilus-shaped compotes on the left and right. In 1809, Wedgwood introduced the varie-gated luster glaze consisting of a "solution of gold with a little tin mixed with sweet wort & laid on with a feather." After firing, the glaze surface was transformed into variations of pink and rose-purple shades with a copper-gold sheen.

MOCHA WARE includes a broad range of utilitarian objects with slip decoration first mass-produced in England in the late 18th century. Shelburne's mocha ware collection is the largest of its kind in an American museum. Numbering over 215 pieces, it is the result primarily of the generosity of two collectors, Mrs. J.C. Rathborne and Edith Blum, as well as Harry T. Peters, a Webb family cousin. Rare examples continue to be added to the collection.

Mocha ware.

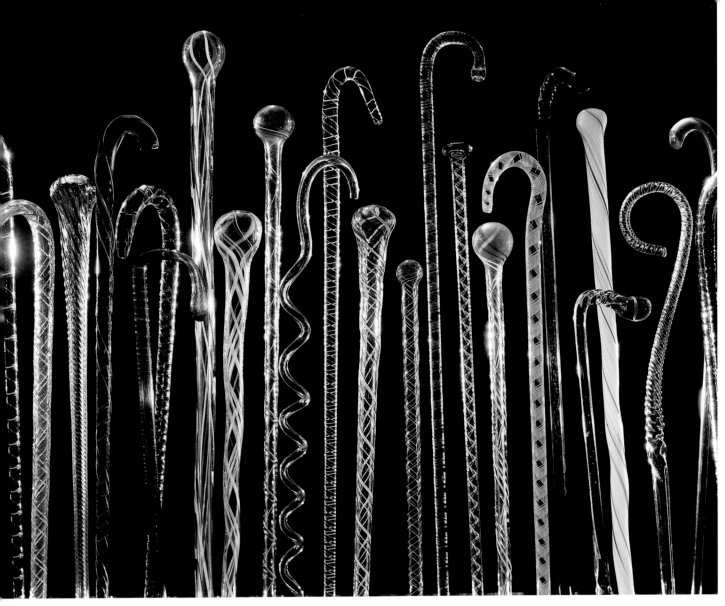

Glass and Pewter

DECORATIVE ARTS collections in Variety Unit showcase pressed and free-blown glass and pewter from Europe and America.

The free-blown glass collection includes decorative pieces such as canes, rolling pins, and witch balls (colorful glass spheres). These whimsies were non-utilitarian objects made at the end of the workday with leftover glass.

Makers Unknown
Glass Canes
American and European
About 1875-1925
Blown or solid glass
Various lengths from 26" to 47"
Gifts of Frederick Thompson and Carmen Edmond-Thompson, 2003
2003-6.1 through 2003.6.24

Shelburne's collection of 167 glass canes is the largest in an American museum. The canes in this photograph were donated to the Museum in 2003.

Israel Trask
Pewter Teapot
Beverly, Massachusetts
1813-18
Pewter with wooden handle
H: 6", W: 10¾", D: 4¼"
Museum purchase, 2004
2004-33

Trained as a silversmith, Israel Trask combined his technical expertise with an understanding of current styles to produce this fashionable oval-shaped neoclassical teapot. The bright cut decoration represents a form of engraving usually seen on silver. The resulting V-shaped facets reflect light at different angles.

Various Makers
Pewter Vessels
European and American
18th and 19th centuries

The Museum's pewter collection of about 250 pieces includes these graduated vessels (left), designed to calculate quantities of alcoholic beverages purchased at taverns and markets. Pewter is an ancient alloy used from Roman times onwards. It is a mixture of several elements (including tin, copper, bismuth, and lead) formed by pouring the molten metal into brass or bronze molds.

Dolls, Dollhouses, and Automata

AT THE AGE OF 10, Electra Webb started collecting dolls her grandmother had dressed. Over the years, the desire to possess many different examples of her favorite playthings led her to accumulate more than 500 dolls, mostly European and American and made between 1760 and 1930. They are exhibited in Variety Unit and, combined with recent acquisitions, comprise one the country's largest and finest doll collections.

The doll galleries also include eight dollhouses and an exhibition of French and American automata (large wind-up toys popular in the late 19th century).

Bru Jne. & Cie
Bébés (Dolls)
Paris and Montreuil-sous-Bois, France
1880-85
Tinted unglazed porcelain swivel head
Left: H: 19 3/4"
Gift of Eleanor Whitmer, 1953
Center: H: 19"
Gift of Mrs. Frederick Moore and Mrs. Lawrence V. Jeffries, 1962
Right: H: 22"
Gift of Electra Havemeyer Webb, 1952-60
20-01-27, 20-01-45, 20-01-125

These bébés are dressed in the height of 19th-century style in silk, satin, velvet, or brocade garments with trimmings of shimmering ribbons and delicate lace.

Probably Gustave Vichy (1839-1904)
Clown Magician
Automaton
French
About 1880
Papier mâché head; linen body; silk, wool, and cotton
Acquired from Mary Whichelow, 1953
22.2.1-2

Maker Unknown
English Gothic Revival Dollhouse
(bedroom detail)
English
Early 19th century
H: 55 3/4", W: 60"
Electra Havemeyer Webb collection gift,
1952-60
30.1-2

This room, with its canopied four-poster bed and miniature portraits, is from one of eight European and American dollhouses on view.

Probably Gustave Vichy (1839-1904)
Clown Walking on Hands
Automaton
French
Late 19th century
Composition head; iron arms and hands; silk and cotton
Acquisition information unknown
22.2.3-9

Shelburne's collection of over 30 Parisian and American automata includes the magician (above at left), and this playful clown. A video in the automata exhibition shows them in operation.

Furniture

Shelburne's furniture collection, which includes pieces from Europe, Canada, and America, are exhibited in several galleries and historic houses throughout the Museum and are the subject of frequent special exhibitions. The collection showcases a range of both high-style and vernacular pieces; its great strength is exceptional American painted furniture. Most pieces date from 1700 to 1900.

Maker Unknown
"Harvard" Chest
Essex County, Massachusetts
1700-25
Painted pine
H: 44 1/8", W: 35 3/8", D: 20 3/4"
Gift of Katharine Prentis Murphy, 1956
3.4-2 (1956-694.8)

In the 19th century, a rare group of chests decorated with red buildings were called "Harvard" chests because the painted images were thought (mistakenly) to represent the brick buildings at Harvard University. The colorful motifs, painted on a black background, were partly inspired by expensive lacquer furniture imported from Asia that was fashionable at the time.

Attributed to John Goddard
Roundabout Chair
Newport, Rhode Island
1760-75
Mahogany, maple, and white pine
H: 31", W: 25 1/2", D: 17 1/2"
Gift of Katharine Prentis Murphy, 1957
3.3-203 (1957-532.1)

The roundabout, or corner, chair was introduced in America in the early 18th century and was one of the most comfortable seats available for a desk. Its two backrests are set at right angles, and its broad, low arms allowed a writer to draw the chair under the fall front of a secretary desk while retaining elbow support.

Elizabeth Paine Lombard (b. 1798), painter
Chamber Table
Bath, Maine
1816
Painted maple and pine
Inscribed in pencil on drawer: *Elizabeth Paine Lombard Feb 1816*
H: 33 1/2", W: 32 1/4", D: 16 3/4"
Purchased from Mrs. Dexter R. Hunneman, 1960
3.6-61 (1960-85)

At the end of the 18th century, ornamental painting — like sampler making — became part of the curriculum in girls' schools. Such skills were thought to be neces-sary for the education of an accomplished woman. Elizabeth Lombard decorated this table with landscapes, shells, seaweed, birds, leaves, and a basket of fruit when she was 18.

Beach Lodge and Beach Gallery

BEACH LODGE houses mainly hunting trophies, and Beach Gallery exhibits Native American artifacts and art of the American West. The adjacent log buildings were built on site in 1960 to evoke an Adirondack hunting camp. They are named for William and Mary Beach, hunting companions of the Webbs and donors of much of the art in Beach Gallery.

Electra Webb's passion for collecting was perhaps rivaled only by her enthusiasm for big-game hunting. Beach Lodge displays many of her trophies — including bear, elk, and moose — as well as hunting boats and artifacts from the Webb family camp in New York's Adirondack Mountains.

In Beach Gallery are landscape and wildlife paintings of western North America by Carl Rungius (1869-1959) and Sydney Mortimer Laurence (1865-1940), among others. Also on view are Native American artifacts, including dugout canoes, pottery, and exceptional examples of beadwork.

Beach Lodge (left and right).

A wall of hunting trophies in Beach Lodge, including an Alaskan brown bear (center) that Electra Webb shot in 1939.

The Museum's collections in Beach Gallery include Native American beadwork.

Carl Rungius (1869-1959)
Bow Lake, Alberta
1923
Oil on canvas
H: 16", W: 20"
Gift of Mr. and Mrs. William N. Beach, 1960
27.1.2-143

American Paintings

THE MUSEUM'S 19th-century American paintings were one of the last major collections to be assembled at Shelburne. Most were purchased in the late 1950s, and today there are over 400 pictures.

John Frederick Peto (1854-1907)
Ordinary Objects in the Artist's Creative Mind
1887
Oil on canvas
Signed lower left: *John F. Peto/1887*
H: 55 ¼", W: 32 ¹¹/₁₆"
Purchased from Maxim Karolik, 1959
27.1.3-19 (1959-265.33)

The artist creates an autobiographical landscape in this painting, which is one of Peto's largest and most ambitious. The painting palette and cornet, symbols of the artist's occupations, are centrally placed and surrounded by objects that allude to his world.

Winslow Homer (1836-1910)
Milking
About 1875
Oil on canvas
H: 15 ½", W: 22 ¾"
Purchased from Eunice Chambers, 1960
27.1.7-11 (1960-197)

Perhaps the most celebrated American painter of the 19th century, Winslow Homer enjoyed critical acclaim throughout his career.

George Henry Durrie (1820-63)

Winter in the Country: A Cold Morning
1862
Oil on canvas
H: 25 ⅛", W: 35 ½"
Given in memory of Mr. and Mrs. P.H.B.
Frelinghuysen by their children, 1963
27.1.2-112 (1963-197.2)

George Henry Durrie was born in New Haven, Connecticut. In his later years, he primarily painted winter landscapes depicting a romantic nostalgia for rural life.

Charles Deas (1818-67)

The Death Struggle
1845
Oil on canvas
Signed lower left: *C Deas 1845*
H: 30", W: 25"
Purchased from Maxim Karolik, 1959
27.1.5-18 (1959-265.16)

This was an extremely popular painting when it was exhibited at the National Academy of Design in New York City in the mid-1840s, when Americans had an insatiable appetite for depictions of the uncharted wilderness of the West.

Edward Lamson Henry (1841-1919)

A Lover of Old China
1889
Oil on academy board
Signed lower right: *E. L. Henry 89*
H: 14", W: 12"
Museum purchase, 1959
27.1.7-2

The artist described the picture this way: "Finding rare examples in the lady's cupboard, the gentleman in this picture was Richard Ely, cor. 5th Avenue and 35th St. The old Lady was Mrs. Livingston Murray (aunt of the artist's wife) & who lived to nearly 101 years of age."

**Severin Roesen
(d. about 1871)**
Ecstatic Fruit
1852
Oil on canvas
Signed lower left:
S. Roesen/1852
H: 34", W: 44"
Acquisition information
unknown
27.1.3-5

Roesen specialized in still lifes with flowers, and he sold several to the American Art Union in New York City to be reproduced as lithographic prints. In this picture, Roesen's elaborate composition indicates that he relied on baroque still lifes of the 17th century as sources for his art.

Washington Allston (1779-1843)
Morning in Italy: Classical Landscape
About 1815
Oil on canvas
H: 16 3/8", W: 20 1/2"
Purchased from Maxim Karolik, 1958
27.1.2-83 (1958-309.1)

Allston was one of the first Americans to practice landscape painting. This view was inspired by the paintings of Claude Lorrain (1600-82), a French artist who lived and painted in Italy.

Thomas Cole (1801-48)
View of the Arno
1838
Oil on wood panel
Signed lower right: *T. Cole/1838*
H: 17", W: 25 1/4"
Purchased from Maxim Karolik, 1957
27.1.2-57 (1957-690.29)

Cole painted this view of the Arno, which flows through Florence, after a trip to Italy. The reverse of the picture bears evidence of mixed pigments, which suggests that the wood may once have served as a makeshift palette.

Jasper Francis Cropsey (1823-1900)

Country Lane to Greenwood Lake

1846

Oil on canvas

Signed lower left: *J. F. Cropsey, 1846*

H: 39 1/8", W: 60"

Purchased from Maxim Karolik, 1959

27.1.2-92 (1959-265.15)

Cropsey first began painting Greenwood Lake, a suburban paradise on the New Jersey-New York border, in 1843. The lake was easily accessible from New York City, where the artist lived, and soon became a favorite place to paint. Cropsey's work in this manner brought him financial success and critical acclaim.

Martin Johnson Heade (1819-1904)

Brazilian Hummingbirds

1866

Oil on canvas

Signed lower left: *M.J.H. 66*

H: 13 11/16", W: 12 1/16"

Purchased from Maxim Karolik, 1959

27.1.5-21 (1959-265.19)

Heade intended to publish a book about hummingbirds with color illustrations. He sent paintings from Rio de Janeiro to M&N Hanhart, a leading lithographic printing firm in London. Unable to find financial support, Heade was forced to abandon the plan.

Anna Mary Robertson (Grandma) Moses (1860-1961)

Old Home

1957

Oil on masonite

Signed lower right: *Moses.*

Inscribed: *To my Dear friend Electra Havemeyer Webb Merry Christmas 1957 Grandma Moses*

H: 11¼", W: 15¼"

Gift of the artist to Electra Havemeyer Webb, 1957

27.1.2-25

For most of her life, Moses lived in New York State near the Vermont border in picturesque hillside villages that became the basis for her pictures. Moses was 67 when she began painting in 1927 after her husband's death. In 1939, art collector Louis Caldor saw her work displayed in a local drugstore window. Caldor's discovery led to her first exhibition the next year in New York City.

Andrew Wyeth (1917-   )

Soaring

1942-50

Tempera on masonite

Signed lower right: *Andrew Wyeth*

H: 48", W: 87"

Purchased from Maxim Karolik, 1961

27.2.5-3 (1961-186.6)

Wyeth started this picture in 1942 but left it unfinished until 1950, when Lincoln Kirstein encouraged the artist to complete it and sell it to him. The birds are turkey vultures.

Erastus Salisbury Field (1805-1900)
The Garden of Eden
About 1865
Oil on canvas
H: 35", W: 41 ½"
Gift of Electra and Dunbar Bostwick, 1959
27.1.2-86 (1959-266)

Adam and Eve live in a state of blissful innocence before disobeying God's command not to eat the forbidden fruit.
The Tree of Knowledge is positioned close to the center of the painting.

Ogden Minton Pleissner (1905-83)
Blue Boat on the Ste Anne 1958
1958
Watercolor on paper
Signed lower left: *Pleissner*
H: 17 ¼", W: 27 ½"
Gift of the Estate of Ogden Pleissner, 1986
27.22.3-195 (1986-26.162)

Ogden Pleissner

Shelburne's collection of 20th-century paintings is dominated by some 600 works by Ogden Pleissner (1905-83). In Pleissner Gallery about 40 paintings and drawings are exhibited on a rotating basis, and the contents of the artist's Manchester, Vermont studio are installed there in his recreated studio (below). One of Pleissner's primary subjects was sport, mostly hunting and fishing scenes.

Quilts

SHELBURNE'S MORE THAN 400 American-made historic quilts form the largest and finest museum collection in the country. Most of the quilts were made between 1800 and 1900. The collection continues to grow through gifts and purchases, and the Museum's quilts are known internationally for their exceptional artistic quality.

Kathryn Cox Williams
Williams Family Quilt
Probably made in Ohio
Dated 1873
Appliquéd, pieced, and embroidered cotton, linen, and silk
H: 93 ¾", W: 93 ⅛"
Museum purchase, 2001
2001-24

The Conestoga wagon near the center is embroidered with the inscription "N.A. Williams, 1873." According to family history, the quilt commemorates the 1871 marriage of Newton Allen Williams (who as a boy had traveled overland with his father to Oregon) and Kathryn Cox.

Attributed to a member of the Ridgley family
Chintz Floral Quilt
Baltimore, Maryland
Early 19th century
Printed, appliquéd, and quilted cotton
H: 104 1/2", W: 80"
Museum purchase, 1954
10-145 (1954-492)

The flowers, which include lilies and roses, have been cut from high-quality European-made chintzes. The white ground of each block has been expertly quilted with scrolling branches that shadow the bouquets of flowers.

Maker Unknown
Scenes of Childhood Crib Quilt
Probably made in New York
About 1872
Embroidered, appliquéd, and printed cotton and drawing in ink
H: 38 1/4", W: 34 3/4"
Museum purchase, 2002
2002-37

The appliquéd figures are based on images published in Peterson's Magazine *in April 1872. The vignettes have the inscriptions: "Here's some more sins in my pocket," "Gran-Pa ride first," and "Dolly is sick."*

Unknown Mennonite Maker
Concentric Squares Quilt
Lancaster County, Pennsylvania
Early 20th century
Pieced and quilted cotton
H: 80", W: 80"
Museum purchase, 1988
10-671 (1988-52.6)

The alternating red and slate blue borders create an extraordinary visual dynamic. The red is beautifully quilted with diamonds, and the blue has cables.

Carrie M. Carpenter (b. 1835)
Sunflower Quilt
Northfield, Vermont
19th century
Inscribed in ink on back: *Carrie M. Carpenter*
Appliquéd and quilted cotton
H: 77 ½" W: 84"
Gift of Ethel Washburn, 1987
10-651 (1987-19)

The tall sunflowers were probably inspired by the 19th-century design vocabulary of the Arts and Crafts movement.

Maker Unknown
Eight-Point Stars Quilt
New England
1790-1820
Pieced and quilted wool
H: 86", W: 103"
Acquisition information unknown
10-740

Hooked Rugs, Samplers, and Coverlets

SHELBURNE MUSEUM'S approximately 300 19th- and 20th-century hooked rugs constitute one of the largest museum collections in the country. Electra Webb took a great interest in hooked rugs, using them extensively to decorate her Vermont and Long Island homes and exhibiting them in the Museum's Hat and Fragrance Textile Gallery.

A highlight of Shelburne's hooked rugs collection is the statehood series by Molly Nye Tobey (1893-1984). Tobey made 50 — one for each state and bearing her own artistic vision of the state's identity — in the 1940s and '50s. The series is a remarkable work of 20th-century American folk art and a masterpiece of rug hooking.

The Museum's textile collections also include about 200 woven coverlets and over 100 embroidered samplers, so named because they provided examples of the needlework skills of young women. One outstanding piece is a silk work made by Mary Eaton in 1763 (opposite, above).

Harry Tyler
Doublecloth Jacquard Loom Coverlet
Jefferson County, New York
1840
Cotton and wool
H: 83", W: 74"
Museum purchase, 1962
10-420 (1962-36)

Mary Eaton
Sampler
1763
Silk embroidered on linen
H: 14 3/4", W: 12 1/2"
Acquisition information unknown
8.2-47

Molly Nye Tobey (1893-1984)
Indiana
Hooked Rug
Massachusetts
Burlap, canvas, and wool
H: 35 1/2", W: 53"
Gift of Joel Tobey, Jonathan Tobey, and
Joshua Tobey, 1991
9-M-82.14

Folk Art Sculpture and Paintings

THE NATION'S premier collection of American folk art is shown in Stagecoach Inn, a 1783 building moved to the grounds from nearby Charlotte, Vermont in 1949. The collection comprises a wide range of forms, including cigar store figures, ship's carvings, trade signs, weather vanes, whirligigs, and paintings. These pieces were often utilitarian and made outside the prevailing conventions of fine art. They were first considered art — and therefore collectable — about 100 years ago.

The northwest gallery, one of nine rooms exhibiting folk art in Stagecoach Inn, includes weather vanes, whirligigs, paintings, and sculpture.

Stagecoach Inn.

Maker Unknown
Spinning Woman
Whirligig
Late 19th century
Carved and painted wood
H: 28", W: 23 ½", D: 22 ½"
Purchased from Edith
Halpert, Downtown Gallery,
1953
FT-71

Spinning Woman *is one of the finest surviving 19th-century whirligigs. No record of its origin exists, but it probably was made as a trade sign for a New England yarn store.*

Henry Leach, Cushing & White Co.
Liberty
Weather Vane Pattern
Waltham, Massachusetts
1879
Carved and painted wood
H: 45 ½", W: 39", D: 13"
Purchased by Electra Havemeyer Webb from Edith Halpert, Downtown Gallery, 1941
FW-104

Because this piece is larger than most weather vanes and made of wood, it was thought for many years to have been a ship's carving.

Edward Hicks (1780-1849)
Penn's Treaty with the Indians
About 1840
Oil on canvas
H: 25", W: 30 1/2"
Purchased from Edith Halpert,
Downtown Gallery, 1953
27.1.6-1

Edward Hicks was a devout Quaker, and the act of peaceful and fair compromise as exemplified here was one of his fundamental values. Hicks trained as a sign painter, and the bold outlines, bright colors, and decorative lettering are typical of trade signs.

PENNS TREATY with the INDIANS, made 1681 with out an Oath, and never broken. The foundation of Religious and Civil LIBERTY, in the U.S. of AMERICA

Maker Unknown
George Washington on Horseback
Early 19th century
Carved and painted wood, leather, and brass
H: 23", W: 22 1/2", D: 7"
Purchased by Electra Havemeyer Webb from
Edith Halpert, Downtown Gallery, and antiques
dealer Mary Allis, 1943
FM-3

In 1943, folk art dealer Edith Halpert wrote that this piece was "one of the most important sculptures discovered in the folk art tradition." It remains one of the most widely known and highly regarded examples of folk art sculpture.

Maker Unknown
Fish with Flag
Trade Sign Fragment
Found in central New York
19th century
Painted wood and sheet iron
H: 34", W: 61", D: ³/₄"
Purchased from The Old Print Shop, New York City, date unknown
FT-80

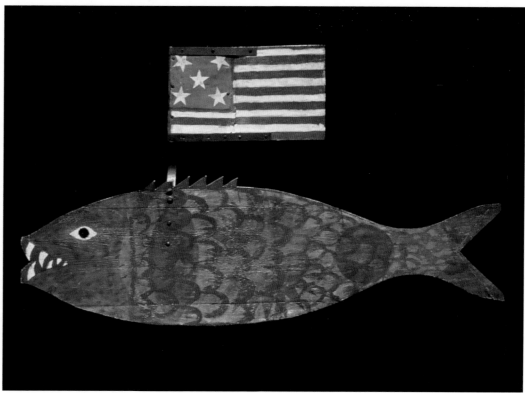

Fish with Flag was probably part of a trade sign for an inn or tavern but survives now only as a fragment. Apart from its New York State origins, nothing is known about this piece.

William Matthew Prior (1806-73)
Little Girl from Maine
1846
Oil on canvas
Inscribed on back: *Painted By Wm. M. Prior. East Boston/April 1846/Value $20.00*
H: 35 ⁹/₁₆"; W: 28 ⁵/₈"
Gift of Dr. and Mrs. Fletcher McDowell, 1959
27.1.1-72 (1959-13.2)

Inscribed on the back of the portrait is "Value $20.00," significantly more than the $2.92 the artist advertised for less finished paintings. Prior probably charged more for this portrait because it is full length, the face is highly detailed, and a toy, book, and landscape background are included.

William Matthew Prior (1806-73)
Mrs. Nancy Lawson
1843
Oil on canvas
Signed lower right: *Nancy Lawson, May 11 1843/W.M. Prior*
H: 30", W: 24 13/16"
Purchased from Maxim Karolik, 1959
27.1.1-124

William Matthew Prior (1806-73)
William Lawson
1843
Oil on canvas
Signed lower right: *W. Lawson, May 2nd 1843/W.M. Prior*
H: 30", W: 24 13/16"
Purchased from Maxim Karolik, 1959
27.1.1-125

Prior traveled throughout New England painting portraits before settling in Boston in 1839. Lawson was listed as a merchant in Boston's People of Color directories of 1841 and 1850.

Warren Gould Roby (1834-97)
Mermaid
Weather Vane
Wayland, Massachusetts
About 1875
Carved pine and metal
H: 22 1/2", W: 52 1/2", D: 4 1/2"
Acquisition information unknown
FW-47

Warren Roby trained as a coppersmith and became a successful businessman buying and selling copper and other metals. He carved this one-of-a-kind weather vane for the barn of his summer home in Wayland, Massachusetts.

Maker Unknown

Pisces

Weather Vane

Originally from New York

1850-75

Painted metal

H: 59 1/4", W: 48 1/4", D: 1 1/4"

Purchased from Edith Halpert, Downtown Gallery, 1951

FW-33

This vane is thought to be a representation of Pisces from the sign of the Zodiac, symbolized here as two fish swimming in opposite directions. The simplicity of the forms and the piece's worn painted surface are striking visual qualities.

Maker Unknown

Sandy the Scotsman

Cigar Store Figure

About 1875

Carved and painted wood

H: 85", W: 28", D: 26"

Purchased by Electra Havemeyer Webb, probably from Sidney Scharlin, 1939

FT-20

This figure stood outside Sidney Scharlin's snuff factory at 113 Division Street in New York City from 1873 until 1938.

Decoys

SHELBURNE MUSEUM'S collection of wildfowl decoys is recognized as the finest and most comprehensive of its kind in the United States. Over 900 works comprise the collection, which is exhibited in Dorset House, a gracious 1832 Greek Revival home from Dorset, Vermont.

Wooden decoys, essential hunting tools in North America for hundreds of years, are in many cases exquisitely crafted works of folk art. The Museum's collection emphasizes outstanding carved and painted pieces as well as regional style differences. Decoys from Maine, Long Island, Chesapeake Bay, Illinois, Quebec, and several other locales are on view.

Anthony Elmer Crowell (1862-1951), one of the most revered American decoy makers, is well represented in Shelburne's collection. A classic example of Crowell's finest work is *Black Duck*, made about 1920. Other prominent decoy makers represented in the collection include Gus Wilson, Harry Shourdes, and Shang Wheeler.

Painted fish decoys, used in ice and spear fishing, are increasingly recognized as significant works of folk art. Shelburne Museum's collection includes several examples from Canada and the Upper Midwest states.

Anthony Elmer Crowell (1862-1951)
Black Duck
Decoy
East Harwich, Massachusetts
About 1920
Carved and painted wood
H: 7 1/2": W: 16 1/2": D: 5 3/4"
Acquisition information unknown
FD 4-43

Dorset House.

A grouping of fish decoys carved and painted about 1930 by various makers (including Oscar Peterson, Art Repp, Manfred Caughell, and Abraham de Hate) in and around Cadillac, Michigan.

A grouping of shorebirds carved about 1900 by Harry Shourdes (1871-1920) of Tuckerton, New Jersey.

Circus Building, Figures, and Posters

The Circus Building is an ingenious horseshoe-shaped structure, one-tenth of a mile long, designed to exhibit collections of carved miniature circuses, carousel figures, and circus posters.

Inside are early 20th-century carousel figures and two miniature circuses: the Roy Arnold Circus Parade and the Kirk Bros. Circus. Hardwick, Vermont native Roy Arnold and four assistants carved the circus parade over 30 years (1925-55). Its nearly 4,000 one-inch-to-one-foot scale figures include a myriad of animals, clowns, acrobats, and circus wagons in a grand parade that stretches over 500 feet.

The Kirk Bros. Circus is a 35,000-piece carved miniature three-ring circus with audience, significant portions of which are exhibited at the entrance of Circus Building. Edgar Kirk (1891-1956) fashioned the figures over 40 years using only a treadle jigsaw and penknife. The end product is a highly imaginative tour de force that consistently ranks among Shelburne Museum's most popular exhibitions.

The Circus Building also features 40 carousel figures made from about 1895 to 1902 by the Gustav Dentzel Carousel Company of Philadelphia, Pennsylvania. Dentzel's figures set the standard for quality, boasting exquisite painting and the finest craftsmanship in the field.

The circus collections include over 500 posters dating from 1870 to 1940. Distinctive for their bright coloring, the posters advertised Barnum and Bailey, Ringling Brothers, and other major shows. Although not on permanent view, the posters are featured periodically in special exhibitions.

Ringling Bros and Barnum & Bailey Circuses
Silk-Screened Poster
About 1930
H: 42", W: 28"
Gift of Harry T. and Natalie Peters, 1959
27.4-178

Center ring, Kirk Bros. Circus.

Daniel Muller (1872-1952),
Gustav Dentzel Carousel Company
Tiger
Carousel Animal
Philadelphia, Pennsylvania
About 1902
H: 53"; W: 80"; D: 32"
Museum purchase, 1952
FC-7

Carousel

Outside Circus Building, sited in the cradle of the gallery's horseshoe, is an operating 1920s carousel made by the Allan Herschell Company of North Tonawanda, New York. Rides on the carousel, accompanied by circus music, are enormously popular, particularly with young children and families.

Daniel Muller (1872-1952),
Gustav Dentzel Carousel Company
Horse
Carousel Animal
Philadelphia, Pennsylvania
About 1902
H: 59"; W: 65"; D: 12"
Museum purchase, 1952
FC-7

Tools and Working Exhibitions

THE MUSEUM'S extensive collection of 18th- and 19th-century tools is exhibited in Shaker Shed, an 1840 structure moved to Shelburne in 1951 from a Shaker community in Canterbury, New Hampshire. On display are hundreds of woodworking tools, cobbler and harness-maker tools, baskets, and a variety of metal and wooden housewares. Part of Shaker Shed is exhibited as a 19th-century cobbler's shop.

Three working exhibitions include demonstrations of essential early-American trades. The Blacksmith Shop, built about 1800 in Shelburne, was moved to the Museum in 1955 and features forge work demonstrating the art and skill of blacksmithing. The Printing Shop exhibits a range of 19th- to early 20th-century presses common to New England print shops, including a rare 1820s hand press operated for Museum visitors. The Weaving Shop showcases several barn-frame looms. The highlight is a rare operating 1890s Jacquard loom.

Blacksmith Shop features blacksmithing demonstrations and displays of tools.

Blacksmith Shop.

Planes and other woodworking tools are exhibited in Shaker Shed.

Shaker Shed.

The 1890s Jacquard loom, a triumph of 19th-century technology used for weaving complex floral and mosaic patterns, is one of only two public examples in operation in the country.

The Brick House

THE BRICK HOUSE was the Vermont home of Electra Webb and her husband James Watson Webb from 1913 to 1960. Originally an early-19th-century farmhouse, the abandoned building was given to the Webbs as a wedding gift. Over the years, they expanded it into a 40-room Colonial Revival masterpiece.

The Brick House was first used as a family retreat for fox hunting, but as Mrs. Webb's collections grew she used its rooms to experiment with different displays of antiques that were later transferred in larger scale to Shelburne Museum. Her combinations of early-American furniture and textiles, English ceramics, historic wallpapers, and a range of folk, fine, and decorative arts influenced major collectors of the period, including Henry Francis du Pont.

The Brick House is unique both as a historically significant example of the Colonial Revival style and as a rare surviving home of a major American museum founder. The property's designation as an official Save America's Treasures® project recognizes its national importance. The Brick House opened to public tours in 2004 after extensive preservation work.

The Brick House.

The first-floor hall of the Brick House with Vermont pewter, hooked rugs, and a reproduced historic wallpaper used by Mrs. Webb.

The Brick House dining room.

View of Lake Champlain and the Adirondack Mountains from the Brick House.